70

Jaguars

by Helen Frost

Consulting Editor: Gail Saunders-Smith, Ph.D.

Consultant: Tammy Quist, President
The Wildcat Society

Pebble Books

an imprint of Capstone Press
Mankato, Minnesota

Pebble Books are published by Capstone Press
151 Good Counsel Drive, P.O. Box 669, Mankato, Minnesota 56002
http://www.capstone-press.com

1 2 3 4 5 6 07 06 05 04 03 02

Library of Congress Cataloging-in-Publication Data
Frost, Helen, 1949–
    Jaguars/by Helen Frost.
    p. cm.—(Rain forest animals)
    Includes bibliographical references (p. 23) and index.
    Summary: Simple text and photographs present the lives of jaguars that live
in rain forests in Central and South America.
    ISBN 0-7368-1193-1
    1. Jaguar—Juvenile literature. [1. Jaguar.] I. Title. II. Series.
QL737.C23 F76 2002
599.75'5—dc21   20013005063

Note to Parents and Teachers

The Rain Forest Animals series supports national science standards
related to life science. This book describes and illustrates jaguars
that live in the rain forest. The photographs support early readers in
understanding the text. The repetition of words and phrases helps
early readers learn new words. This book also introduces early
readers to subject-specific vocabulary words, which are defined in
the Words to Know section. Early readers may need assistance to
read some words and to use the Table of Contents, Words to Know,
Read More, Internet Sites, and Index/Word List sections of
the book.

Table of Contents

Jaguars are large cats.

Cats are mammals.

9

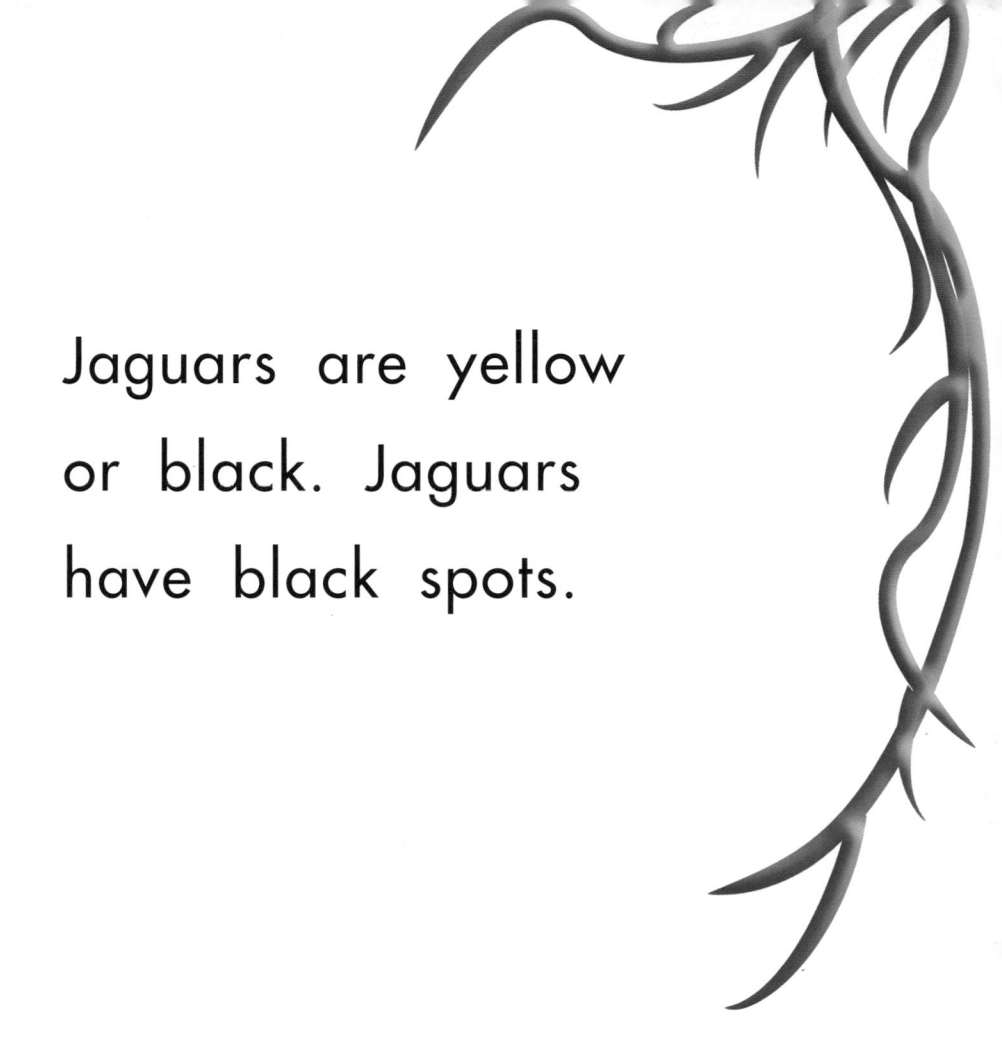

Jaguars are yellow or black. Jaguars have black spots.

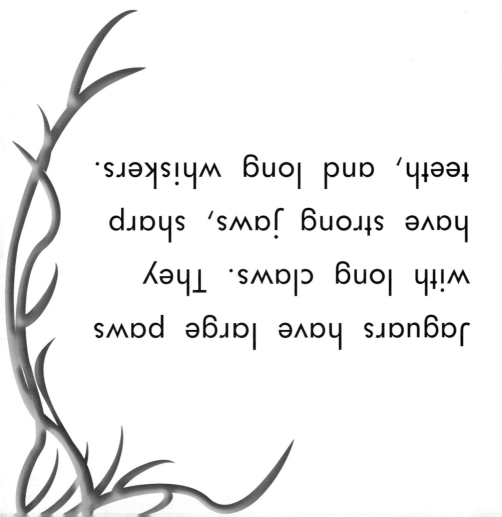

Jaguars have large paws with long claws. They have strong jaws, sharp teeth, and long whiskers.

■ places jaguars live

Jaguars live in
the tropical rain forest
in South America.

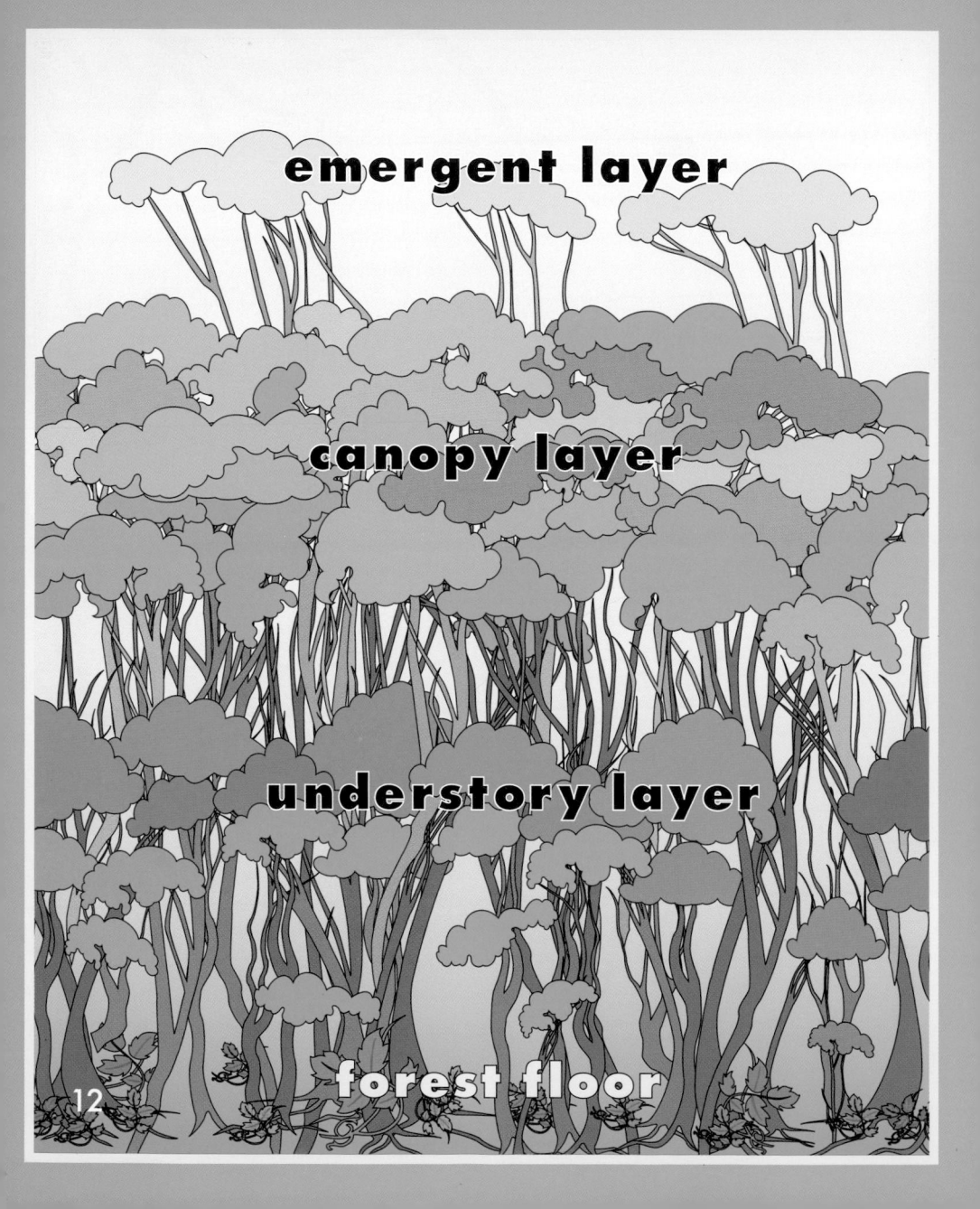

emergent layer

canopy layer

understory layer

forest floor

12

Jaguars roam across
the forest floor.

Jaguars walk along
the ground. They climb
low branches.

Jaguars swim in rivers.

Jaguars often hunt prey at dusk. They eat peccaries, rodents, and fish.

jaguar eating a peccary

Jaguars sleep
on tree branches.

Words to Know

dusk—the time of day after sunset when it is almost dark; jaguars can see well in the dark.

forest floor—the bottom part of the rain forest; almost no sunlight reaches the forest floor.

mammal—a warm-blooded animal with a backbone; mammals have hair or fur; female mammals feed milk to their young.

peccary—an animal that is related to the pig; the peccary is active at dusk.

prey—an animal that is hunted by another animal for food

spot—a marking on the body of an animal; jaguars have small black spots inside a ring of large black spots.

tropical rain forest—a dense area of trees where rain falls almost every day; the Amazon tropical rain forest is in South America.

Read More

Lalley, Pat. *Jaguars.* Animals of the Rain Forest. Austin, Texas: Steadwell Books, 2000.

Vogel, Elizabeth. *Jaguars.* Big Cats. New York: PowerKids Press, 2002.

Woods, Theresa. *Jaguars.* Nature Books. Chanhassen, Minn.: Child's World, 2001.

Internet Sites

Jaguar
http://www.kidsplanet.org/factsheets/jaguar.html

Jaguar
http://www.wildcatsociety.org/catalog/
big%20cats/jaguar.html

Jaguar: Lord of the Mayan Jungle
http://www.oneworldjourneys.com/jaguar/
index.html

Index/Word List

black, 7
branches, 15, 21
cats, 5
claws, 9
climb, 15
dusk, 19
forest floor, 13
ground, 15
hunt, 19
jaws, 9

large, 5, 9
live, 11
long, 9
low, 15
mammals, 5
paws, 9
prey, 19
rain forest, 11
rivers, 17
roam, 13

sharp, 9
sleep, 21
South America, 11
spots, 7
strong, 9
swim, 17
teeth, 9
whiskers, 9
yellow, 7

Word Count: 78
Early-Intervention Level: 12

Editorial Credits
Sarah Lynn Schuette, editor; Jennifer Schonborn, production designer and interior illustrator; Linda Clavel and Heidi Meyer, cover designers; Kia Bielke, interior illustrator; Kimberly Danger and Mary Englar, photo researchers

Photo Credits
Bruce Coleman, Inc., 1, 6 (bottom), 14, 16, 18, 20
Digital Vision, 10 (background)
International Stock LLC/Greg Johnston, cover, 6 (top)
Tom and Pat Leeson, 4, 8

The author thanks the children's section staff at the Allen County Public Library in Fort Wayne, Indiana, for research assistance.